EXPLORE
my world

Butterflies

By Marfé Ferguson Delano

NATIONAL
GEOGRAPHIC
KiDS

WASHINGTON, D.C.

Look, butterflies!

Fluttering, floating, zigzagging by, they flash like jewels in the sunlit sky. They flit over fields and wander through woods.

They glide into gardens
and dance through deserts.

What are butterflies looking for? Flowers to feed on. When a butterfly lands, it tastes the flower with the tips of its feet!

This flower tastes sweet. Deep inside it is a sugary liquid called nectar. The butterfly unrolls a long tube on its head and pokes it into the flower.

Slurp!

The butterfly uses the tube like a straw to suck up the nectar.

9

What's for Lunch?

How does a butterfly taste its food?

Do you think dead bugs taste yucky or yummy?

Some butterflies drink nectar from almost any flower. Others are picky eaters. They only feed on certain flowers.

What's your favorite— fresh apples or rotten ones?

A few butterflies prefer to dine on rotting fruit or even dead bugs! Here are some butterflies with their favorite foods.

It's raining. To keep dry, a butterfly folds up its wings and perches below a leaf.

At night, a butterfly hangs upside down to sleep.

To warm up in the morning, a butterfly spreads its wings wide and soaks up the sun. A butterfly's life may seem fancy-free, but any moment…

Swoop!

A hungry monkey might sneak up and snatch it!

A mouse might munch it!
A bird might nab it!
A lizard might zap it!

How can butterflies stay safe? Some hide by blending in with the world around them.

Some have spots on their wings that look like eyes. Eyespots scare away enemies. BOO!

A Rainbow of Colors

A butterfly's wings are covered with thousands of tiny, powdery scales. These scales create the insect's beautiful colors and patterns.

Each scale is a single color.

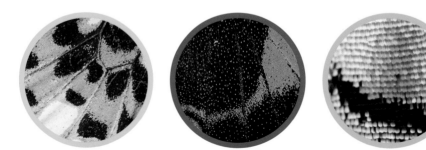

Here are some butterflies from around the world. How many of them have eyespots?

small tortoiseshell butterfly
Eurasia

blue morpho butterfly
South, Central America

common buckeye
butterfly
North America

common Mormon
butterfly
Asia

blue pansy butterfly
Asia, Australia

Pallas's fritillary butterfly
Eurasia

A mother butterfly flies from plant to plant, tasting them with her feet. She's looking for one her babies can eat. When she finds the right plant, she lays her eggs on it.

The eggs hatch and out creep the babies. The babies are tiny caterpillars, very hungry caterpillars!

A caterpillar gobbles up the plant it's on. It eats and eats. It grows and grows.

Wriggle!

It grows so big its skin splits. The caterpillar wriggles out of it. Then it gets too big for its new skin. Again and again this happens. Eat, grow, split, wriggle.

One day the caterpillar hangs upside down from a leaf or twig. It makes a hard, thin shell around its body. The shell is called a chrysalis.

Inside the chrysalis something amazing happens. The caterpillar changes into a butterfly!

After days or weeks, the chrysalis splits open. Out crawls the new butterfly.

The butterfly's wings are crumpled and wet. But soon they straighten out and dry.

Fly, butterfly!

Now the butterfly is ready to take off, to fly, to flash like a jewel in the sunlit sky.

From Egg to Butterfly

Egg

1

How many eggs do you count on this leaf?

Caterpillar

2

How do you think this caterpillar would feel if you touched it?

All butterflies go through four very different stages. Here is the life cycle of a blue morpho butterfly.

Chrysalis

3

What big change happens in this stage?

Butterfly

4

Guess what's on the other side of these wings: Eyespots!

Spy a Butterfly!

Some butterflies are very good at hiding in plain sight.
Can you find the butterfly in each picture?

Grow a Butterfly Garden!

You can lure butterflies to your home by planting their favorite flowers in your yard or in pots.

Grow tall plants and short plants.

Plant lots of flowers, so the butterflies can slurp nectar!

Plant brightly colored flowers.

Choose a sunny spot.

What colors do you see in this garden?

Butterfly-Friendly Plants

- milkweed
- butterfly bush
- daisies

- phlox
- joe-pye weed
- coneflowers

- zinnias
- marigolds
- daylilies

For David, with love
—MFD

Editors: Jennifer Emmett and Ariane Szu-Tu
Art Director: Amanda Larsen
Photography Editor: Lori Epstein

National Geographic supports K-12 educators with ELA Common Core Resources. Visit www.natgeoed.org/commoncore for more information.

Trade paperback ISBN: 978-1-4263-1699-9

Reinforced library binding ISBN: 978-1-4263-1700-2

The publisher gratefully acknowledges entomologist Dr. William O. Lamp of the University of Maryland for his expert review of the book.

ILLUSTRATIONS CREDITS

SS: Shutterstock   iS: iStockphoto
Cover, Steven Russell Smith Photos/SS; Back cover, (UP), Steve Taylor ARPS/Alamy; (LO), digitalimagination/iS; 1, digitalimagination/iS; 2-3, DelafrayeNicolas/iS; 4-5, Richard Ellis/Alamy; 6, AttaBoyLuther/iS; 7, Clive Nichols/GAP Photos RM/Getty Images; 8, Awei/SS; 9, Olga Bogatyrenko/SS; 10 (LOLE), SS/PCHT; 10 (UP), Darlyne A. Murawski; 10 (LO), Chris Routledge; 11 (UP), Tracey Whitefoot/Alamy; 11 (LOLE), king_tut/iS; 11 (LORT), Ed Reschke/Photolibrary RF/Getty Images; 12, Vasilieva Tatiana/SS; 13, szefei wong/Alamy; 14, Paul Kennedy/Lonely Planet Images/Getty Images; 15 (UP), W. Perry Conway/Corbis; 15 (CTR), Joe McDonald/Visuals Unlimited/Getty Images; 15 (LO), Stephen Dalton/Minden Pictures/Corbis; 16 (UP), fotogaby/iStockphoto; 16 (LO), Gianna Stadelmyer/SS; 17, Melinda Fawver/SS; 18 (UP), Kirsanov Valeriy Vladimirovich/SS; 18 (CTR), Nikola Rahme/SS; 18 (LOLE), Pan Xunbin/SS; 18 (LOCTR), Pan Xunbin/SS; 18 (LORT), D. Kucharski K. Kucharska/SS; 19 (UPRT), Hannamariah/SS; 19 (UPLE), Steve Taylor ARPS/Alamy; 19 (CTR), Michael Zysman/SS; 19 (LOLE), Matee Nuserm/SS; 19 (LOCTR), HHakim/iS; 19 (LORT), Kirsanov Valeriy Vladimirovich/SS; 20, Manamana/SS; 21, Carol Saunders/Alamy; 22, Martin Page/Photolibrary RM/Getty Images; 23, Cathy Keifer/SS; 24, Thomas Kitchin & Victoria Hurst/First Light/Getty Images; 25, RyanKing999/iS; 26-27, A & J Visage/Alamy; 28 (LE), WILDLIFE GmbH/Alamy; 28 (RT), Survivalphotos/Alamy; 29 (LE), WILDLIFE GmbH/Alamy; 29 (RT), Juniors Bildarchiv GmbH/Alamy; 30 (UPLE), 49pauly/iS; 30 (UPCTR), Andrea Dal Max/SS; 30 (UPRT), Anna Yu/iS; 30 (LOLE), Fabien Monteil/SS; 30 (LOCTR), Wilfried Besler/iS; 30 (LORT), Wilm Ihlenfeld/SS; 31, Dave Bevan/Alamy

BUTTERFLY NAMES BY PAGE NUMBER

Page 1: blue morpho butterfly
Pages 2-3: glasswinged butterflies
Pages 4-5: monarch butterfly
Page 6: monarch butterfly
Page 7: small tortoiseshell butterfly
Page 8: swallowtail butterfly
Page 9: paper kite butterfly
Page 10 (left): plain tiger butterfly
Page 10 (bottom right): comma butterfly
Page 10 (top right): Donella clearwing butterfly
Page 11 (left): Malay lacewing butterfly
Page 11 (bottom right): monarch butterfly
Page 11 (top right): owl butterfly
Page 13: common yellow swallowtail butterfly
Page 15 (top left): monarch butterfly
Page 15 (middle right): swallowtail butterfly
Page 16 (bottom left): blood red glider butterfly
Page 16 (top right): dead leaf butterfly
Page 17: common buckeye butterfly
Page 20: plain tiger butterfly
Page 21: owl butterfly
Page 22: carnation tortrix moth caterpillars
Page 23: monarch caterpillar larva
Page 24: monarch chrysalis
Page 25: plain tiger butterfly
Pages 26-27: monarch butterflies
Page 28 (left): blue morpho eggs
Page 28 (right): blue morpho caterpillar
Page 29 (left): blue morpho chrysalis
Page 29 (right): blue morpho butterfly
Page 30 (top left): emerald swallowtail butterfly
Page 30 (top center): cloudless sulfur butterfly
Page 30 (top right): paper kite butterfly
Page 30 (bottom left): dead leaf butterfly
Page 30 (bottom center): brimstone butterfly
Page 30 (bottom right): gray cracker butterfly

Printed in the United States of America
14/WOR/1

Delano, Marfe Ferguson

Butterflies